Taming the Restless Heart

Gerald Vann, O.P.

Taming
the
Restless Heart

How to Know God's Will
and Dwell in the Peace It Brings

SOPHIA INSTITUTE PRESS®
Manchester, New Hampshire

Taming the Restless Heart: How to Know God's Will and Dwell in the Peace It Brings was first published in 1947 by Sheed and Ward, New York, under the title *His Will Is Our Peace*. This 1999 edition by Sophia Institute Press contains minor editorial revisions to the original text.

On the cover: *Apostles Peter and John hurry to the tomb on the morning of the Resurrection*, by Eugene Burnand, Musee d'Orsay, Paris, France (photograph courtesy of Erich Lessing / Art Resource, New York).

Sophia Institute Press®
Box 5284, Manchester, NH 03108
1-800-888-9344
www.sophiainstitute.com

Nihil obstat: Rev. Bernard Delany, O.P., B.Litt;
George Can. Smith, S.Th.D., Ph.D., *Censor Deputatus*
Imprimatur: E. Morrough Bernard, *Vic. Gen.*
Westminster, June 1, 1946

Library of Congress Cataloging-in-Publication Data

Vann, Gerald, 1906-1963.
    [His will is our peace]
    Taming the restless heart : how to know God's will and dwell in the peace it brings / Gerald Vann.
       p.   cm.
    Originally published: His will is our peace. New York : Sheed and Ward, 1947.
    Includes bibliographical references.
    ISBN 1-928832-03-2 (pbk)
    1. Christian life. 2. God — Will. I. Title.
BV4501.2.V356 1999
248.4'82 — dc21
                                   99-055749

00 01 02 03 10 9 8 7 6 5 4 3 2

Contents

Editor's note: The biblical references in the following pages are based on the Douay-Rheims edition of the Old and New Testaments. Where applicable, quotations have been cross-referenced with the differing numeration in the Revised Standard Version, using the following symbol: (RSV =).

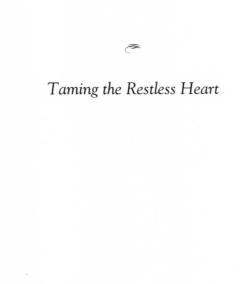

Taming the Restless Heart

Chapter One

*Find peace by
doing God's will*

In His will is our peace. What does it mean? In these sad and troubled days of ours, we must often be driven back to the thought of our Lord's words: "Peace I leave with you; my peace I give unto you."[1] And do we think of them rather ruefully, as of something that, for us at least, must remain an unattainable dream?

Our world has lived through war and all its misery, but even when war is over, there is no peace on earth. Everywhere there is trouble or the threat of trouble. Everywhere there is distress, hunger, and suffering.

How can we be at peace in such a world? But our Lord expressly told us, "Not as the world giveth, do I

---

[1] John 14:27.

give peace."[2] Perhaps we cannot find peace because we look in the wrong place.

What does the world mean by *peace?* One idea of peace is the absence of worries from without: "If only they'd leave me alone," people say. Again, people say, "I shan't rest until I get it," implying that when they have what they want, they will be able to rest; they will be at peace, and thus peace means for them just having what they want. There is no need to underline the instability of any peace of that sort.

We cannot make ourselves immune from external troubles and worries; they flood in on us. We cannot guarantee that what we have we shall keep; we cannot talk of stability of possession when we're on the edge of a volcano.

But it is not thus that our Lord speaks of peace. Remember that it is on the eve of His Passion that He speaks most of peace and of joy. With the saints, too,

[2] Ibid.

it is when they are being tortured and killed that their joy and their peace of soul are most manifest. And we need not look far for the reason. "The fruit of the Spirit is charity, joy, peace . . ."[3] Love is the hunger to live and die for the beloved, and where that hunger is being fulfilled, of course there is joy, of course there is peace; and if the love is great enough and deep enough, no torments will outweigh joy and peace.

In His will is our peace, and it is a peace that nothing can take from us — provided we love enough.

Our Lord spoke of peace as He went to the Cross, and this peace that is His gift is indeed the peace of the Crucified — depending on the Cross, coming from the Cross. We shall not find peace by trying to run away from the horrors and miseries of the world; they will seek us out. We shall find it, on the contrary, as He did — by doing our best to *share* in them, in order, with Him, to help in their healing.

[3] Gal. 5:22.

Taming the Restless Heart

What exactly must we do? We must, first of all, remember that we call God our Father, and that therefore every man and woman in the world is our brother and our sister; in other words, we must feel a sense of responsibility toward them in the same sort of way as we do toward the members of our own family: their sorrows are our sorrows.

Second, we are more than merely involved in the sorrow of the world; we must accept our share of responsibility for it. Suffering is the fruit of sin, and we are sinners; we add to the total force of evil in the world and, therefore, to the total of suffering that it begets. We must start, then, from a sense of responsibility that is based on humility and the sense of sin. Then we must try to go on to accept the situation as it is, the suffering as it is, precisely inasmuch as it is God's *will* that out of all the evil, good should eventually come. And it is in that acceptance that we shall find peace. Why? Because then, through all the turmoil and trouble — yes, and the suffering too — our eyes will be fixed on that infinite, still point which is His unchanging love and compassion, the love and compassion in which all wounds are healed.

⁓

You must fix your gaze on the Lord

"My eyes are ever on the Lord":[4] joy and peace come after love, come out of love, because it is love that makes the soul fix its gaze on God instead of on itself, and want to serve God rather than itself. You know how hardship, drudgery, and pain can become a joy if they express love, if in undergoing them we are serving love. So it is with the saints on the rack and on the scaffold; so it is with the saints who, in company with Christ, have taken on themselves the sins and sorrows of the world: at the deepest level of their hearts, they have known a joy and a peace that no man could take from them, because, in their sufferings, they have known the fulfillment of love.

[4] Cf. Ps. 24:15 (RSV = Ps. 25:15).

Taming the Restless Heart

We let our peace be broken by such littlenesses: a transient worry, a small slight, the aches and pains of the body, the vanities of the soul. These can be enough to make us lose our self-possession, to act as though the ends of the world were come upon us, to grumble against God. We have to be sensible, of course. There are times when the body needs rest and the mind needs relaxation, and if we refuse them, we lessen our power of resistance to these temptations.

But why can they play such havoc with us even when we are well? It is because all too easily they drive our attention wholly inward on ourselves: the aching tooth, the injury done to us by the unkindness of a friend, fill our horizon, and the more we think of them, the larger they loom.

It is just at these times that we need most to con-centrate our gaze on God. "My eyes are ever on the Lord." In the light of that infinity and of the vastness of the pain in which that infinity is involved, how small our private woes appear; and how much easier, too, to offer in love our whole lives to God — including our pain and woes in their right proportions — so that the purposes of His love and His compassion may be fulfilled.

Must we, then, be content with everything as it is, our sins included?

No, of course not: we must remember another saying of our Lord: "I came to bring not peace but the sword"[5] — a sword to cut to pieces our self-complacence, a sword to symbolize the strife between flesh and spirit, between pride and humility, between egoism and love.

The sight of our own sins, the sight of the evil in the world at large, should fire us with a divine discontent — *must* fire us with a divine discontent if there is love in us. But of this, too, it is true to say that it will not destroy our inner peace. Indeed, the greater our determination to make things better with ourselves

[5] Cf. Matt. 10:34.

and with the world, the greater our peace; for the de-termination will be the act of a will fixed in love and worship and hope on the will of God. It will be from Him that we look for the strength we need; we shall be able to say, "With the Lord there is mercy and plentiful redemption," because we shall have started our prayer, "Out of the depths . . ."[6]

It is not easy to acquire this ability to keep our eyes on the Lord, to keep our wills in calm, humble, and joyful union with His will. If we could do it completely, we would ourselves be saints. But we can find out how we are to set about it. And even to have begun is to have achieved some measure of inward peace, for to have begun means to have remembered Christ's words of encouragement and to have been heartened by them: "Let not your heart be troubled, nor let it be afraid."[7]

[6] Cf. Ps. 129:1, 7 (RSV = Ps. 130: 1, 7).
[7] John 14:27.

Chapter Two

*Be attentive to
God's presence*

"My eyes are ever on the Lord":[8] so the psalmist sings; so the saints can truly say. But we know with what little truth we could say it ourselves, we who find such difficulty in resting in God's presence without distraction even when we have set out to pray, and who for such long periods during the day seem to forget Him entirely. And sometimes we fail to realize that we cannot be with God unless we are prepared to fight our way into His presence, unless we are willing to undertake the long and heavy labor of searching for Him.

People sometimes say, "But God is already with us. We've been baptized, and therefore God dwells within us. We have the Holy Eucharist, and Christ is

[8] Cf. Ps. 24:15 (RSV = Ps. 25:15).

our Guest." Yes, but it is one thing to have a guest staying in the house and quite another to get to know that guest. The sacraments give us the radical power of coming to know and love God; they are not magic. The Eucharist means the presence of Christ within us; but unless we make the necessary effort, He must remain the unknown Guest. So St. Teresa[9] tells us that after Communion we must forget about the world and about our own bodies and go deep down into the soul and *find* the presence there within us, and with that presence be still.

How, then, are we to learn to know that presence and live with it?

If we were to consider the answer fully, we would have to think of the whole life of prayer, of our attitude toward creatures, and of the Christian idea of the moral life, for all these things are aspects of the search for God. But let us make a start with one very simple

[9] Possibly St. Teresa of Avila (1515-1582), Carmelite nun and mystic. — ED.

idea, one very simple but overwhelming *fact*, which God's mercy has given us.

⌒

Awareness of God's presence
will help you to love His will

People sometimes say, "Oh, if only our Lord were here in person, how much easier it would all be — if we could see Him and touch Him and listen to His words, how soon we would know Him and how inevitably the thought of Him would be always with us then." But, of course, what we forget — in every practical sense — is that our Lord is here in person and that if we cannot see Him with our eyes, as His disciples saw Him in Palestine, still we can really come to know Him, talk to Him, and listen to Him, if only we make sufficient effort.

And sometimes it is good for us to stop and think: Now, suppose our Lord really did appear, in bodily form as once long ago in Palestine, in my house, my town. Suppose someone came to me with white face and trembling lips and told me that He was there, standing in the house, in a room downstairs. What would I do? Imagine the awe, the shame, yes, perhaps the terror, with which I would go to Him. And yet how I would hope that, in spite of all my sin, He might smile at me as He smiled at those others in Palestine. And if He did, how would I ever forget the happiness of it? And if His eyes were terrible, how would I ever forget that either?

Sometimes it can be useful to think like that, because then we have to go on to tell ourselves: Yes, but He *is* here; that same Man *is* with us — the Man who said the terrible things in the Gospel, the Man who spoke of Hell and eternal loss and torment; and, at the same time, the Man who said the lovely things in the Gospel, the Man who healed the sick, caressed the children, and cleansed and comforted the sinners. It is that same Man who is with us now in the tabernacle, but we forget; we know the fact with our minds, but we know it as we might know some abstract truth, and so the *sense* of His presence grows dim in us, and we act as though it were not true.

What do we lose? Among other things, the ability to make our wills at every moment instantly, lovingly, and joyfully obedient to His will. Think again of that bodily presence into which you were imagining you came. Suppose that He then asked a service of you. Would you be able to hesitate? Would the likely inconveniences, the sufferings perhaps, that it might cause burden you? You would see them against the background of infinity, of infinite love, and, in that blinding fire, they would fade into nothingness. But no, too often we miss what is offered to us.

~

Genuflecting can deepen your love for God's will

Even when we come into His presence in the tabernacle, our thoughts are full of ourselves; our worries and woes are the things that weigh on us. We cannot glimpse the Infinite. That is why anything we can do to impress the sense of that presence on ourselves is of

19

such value. And there is one very simple thing that the Church teaches us to do that can help us greatly if only we do it well: we can learn how to genuflect when we go into church.

To genuflect, to bend the knee: what does it mean? It is a sign of submission, of dependence, of loyalty and service, as of a subject to his king. It means: I recognize that *You* are the important one, not I. It means, in the words of the psalmist, "I am Thy servant, and the son of Thy handmaid."[10] It means, in short, "*Thy* will be done," expressing precisely that union of our will with God's which it is our object to achieve.

Now, we tend, of course, by force of habit, to make our genuflections rather automatically, unreflectingly; they become a matter of routine. But if we do that, we again miss a great opportunity.

In the first place, a genuflection is a sacramental. This means that if it is done with sufficient care and

[10] Ps. 115:16 (RSV = Ps. 116:16).

devotion in mind and will, it can be an occasion of actual grace for us; it can bring us nearer to God. And there is thus a sense in which, like the sacraments, although in a different way, it will effect what it signifies: it will lead to the bringing about in us of a deeper sense of that loving acceptance of God's will which it expresses in symbolic form.

In the second place, we shall, if we are wise, form a conscious habit to counteract the effect of the unconscious effect of routine. We shall choose some phrase that, for us individually, expresses vividly and cogently the sense of worship and of creaturely concentration on God and the will of God,[11] and we shall make our genuflection deliberately enough to allow us to say the phrase in our hearts, with our eyes and our

---

[11] It could be, for example, the words of the publican: "O God, be merciful to me, a sinner" (Luke 18:13); or our Lady's "Behold the handmaid of the Lord" (Luke 1:38); or the words of the apostle Thomas: "My Lord and my God!" (John 20:28); or simply "Thy will be done."

minds on Christ in the tabernacle, addressing the prayer to Him. And so we shall make His presence a reality to ourselves, until perhaps, in time, the sense of that presence becomes habitual with us even when we are not in church; and so the words of the psalmist — "My eyes are ever on the Lord," which is what we aspire to — may begin to be true of our own lives.

"He took to Himself our humanity that He might raise us to His divinity," and, in His pity for our weakness, He has given us even such simple means as these to start us on the way to the mountains of God. We should take them with gladness and humility and hope, knowing that, if only we are faithful in small things, He can do great things in us: "I have raised my eyes to the mountains, from whence help shall come to me."[12]

[12] Ps. 120:1 (RSV = Ps. 121:1).

Chapter Three

Learn to love
creation according
to God's will

If we set out along the road that leads to God, and to the loving union of our will with the will of God, we cannot get far without meeting a dragon.

In the myths of the world, this theme of the hero who sets out on a dark journey and must meet and slay a dragon is recurrent. You find it again in the works of the poets. And all these statements of the theme are statements of what man knows in his deepest self to be the truth about humanity: there is something within us that has to be fought and slain before we can find life. We must, as our Lord told Nicodemus, be born again before we can come to the kingdom of God.[13]

[13] John 3:3.

And what is the dragon? In the Garden of Eden, man tried to shake off the dominion of God and to be his own master, and therefore to make God's creatures *his* things instead of God's. You shall decide, the Devil told them, what is good and what is evil, and so you'll decide for yourselves how you'll make use of things; they'll be *yours*. The firstborn of pride is avarice.

So it is to this day. Every sin is a form of egoism: we set ourselves up as lords of life in defiance of the will and the truth of God. And where creatures are concerned, what does that mean? It means avarice: I want this; I want that; I'm going to use this and that as I think fit. And having tried to eliminate God, we soon find ourselves trying to eliminate our neighbor. We find that greed is a thing that separates, and therefore makes love impossible to us. We turn things into mere utilities — for our pleasure or our profit or our pride. We turn even our friends into utilities in the same way, and so we make it impossible to love them. We can love only ourselves.

What is the result? The things that should have led us to God — the things that He made, and about which His presence clings — are, through our own fault, turned into a distraction from Him. We turn back upon our Baptism. For that was our first dark journey. We go down to the waters of Baptism in order to rise again to the new life, and, in the power of the sacrament, we are freed from the bondage of the dragon of egoism, if only we use the power given to us.

⌒

Created things can lead you to God

And our newfound life as children of God is meant to include a new attitude toward the things that God has made. They are His; we are only stewards for Him when we use and enjoy them. So we must respect them, love them for what they are in themselves and for the praise they give Him, not just for what we get out of them for ourselves. They are meant to help us to God. How? Insofar as we can learn to think of them as belonging to God and loved by God and giving praise to

God, we shall find that they, for their part, will speak to us of God, and we shall join with them in their song of praise.

Do you remember the story of the Abbot Helenus, who, needing a priest for Mass, chartered a crocodile to ferry him across the river in search of one? (But the priest, not being a man of God, not being able to join in the song of praise, fled for his life when he saw the nature of the transport.) Do you remember how St. Francis[14] talked to the birds and shared with them their song and his love? One of the most important qualities that things have is their power of association: if you sometimes take the cat aside and tell it about God — if, to be more literal, you think sometimes as you stroke it how good it was of God to make something so lithe and lovely and to give it to you to look after — then the cat, at other times, will remind you of God, and help you to praise God too.

[14] St. Francis of Assisi (c. 1182-1226), founder of the Franciscan Order.

Things inanimate as well as animate can all speak to us of God, if only we train ourselves. Here as elsewhere we must start in a small way. Choose any particular creature — from a beech tree or a mountain to a blade of grass, from a horse, a dog, or a cat to a bumblebee — and take conscious occasion from them to bless almighty God. You will begin to join in the song of praise. Renew your Baptism every night, as the dark journey of sleep approaches, begging God to make you love things with Him, not against Him — as part of your love for Him, not as a rival to it. That is one step.

Then there are human beings, who in so special a sense can be the habitation of God, and who therefore should speak to us so powerfully of His presence. Again, you have to make the conscious effort of association, and start in a small way with individuals. And perhaps it is useful here to do two things.

First, take someone of whom you are particularly fond and with whom you spend a great deal of your time and share many interests. Talk sometimes to God about them, and sometimes to them about God and the things of God. And sometimes stop and reflect that God made them and loves them and dwells within them, and that it is for you to share with them in the search for God.

Second, take someone whom, on the contrary, you find it hard to like, or some person about whom there is little that is attractive. Again, sometimes make the conscious effort to remind yourself that they, too, come from God and that He loves them. And so about them, too, the presence of God will begin to be discernible.

So with things, with animals, and with human beings, you will have made a beginning. You will have taken the first step toward restoring in your own self something of that family unity and family spirit and family worship which belonged to the world before the Fall. You will have begun to make creatures not a hindrance but a help to God. And finally, you will have done much to defeat and slay the dragon, for if, in your treatment of creatures, you have a sense of God's presence in and about them, and His lordship over them, you will be less inclined to treat them as though they were *your* creatures, less inclined to love them selfishly and in defiance of God's will, less inclined even to love them apart from your love of God. By accepting them lovingly and gratefully from Him when He gives them, you will find it easier to give them back to Him if He asks it of you. Your love will be less grasping and possessive, and therefore more like God's own love. In the end, you will be able to love everything, and the words of our Lord will be verified in you: "Happy are the poor in spirit, for theirs is the kingdom of Heaven."[15]

[15] Matt. 5:3.

Chapter Four

⤳

Fulfill your role in God's plan

"Though I should walk in the valley of darkness," says the psalmist, "yet will I fear no evil: for Thou art with me."[16] If we want to be holy — and happy — we have to learn to love God enough to make our will identical with His, so that when we say, "Thy will be done," we really mean it, not only about this and that but about everything. We need, therefore, a strong sense of and a deep love of God's Providence.

What does it mean to love God's Providence? It does not mean, in the first place, the fatalism that makes no efforts. On the contrary, the efforts that we can make are part of God's plan; events do depend on our free will. Nor does it mean the purely natural

[16] Cf. Ps. 22:4 (RSV = Ps. 23:4).

placidity of temperament that some people enjoy, so that nothing seems able to ruffle their composure. Nor again is it a merely passive resignation, as the word is often understood: a reluctant admission that what can't be cured must be endured.

No, the Lord is our Shepherd. His love has ceaseless and untiring care of us. He is with us. And we are to have faith and trust that His plan is a loving plan — that although things are very black, His wisdom and love and power are there to save and to heal, to bring good out of the evil.

You have your own part in God's plan

A little boy, helping his father with a job of carpentry, will concentrate on some one little thing that his father gives him to do, not seeing how the finished work will emerge from these preliminaries, but content, trusting implicitly that the job will be finished and will be successful. We should do the same with our lives and all the things that make up our lives. God gives us this little bit of His work to do for Him. We ought to have the child's trust that His skill and His love will see the work through, and we should concentrate on our own minute share in it, on doing that well. So we should be saved from that solicitude against which our Lord warns us. He does not tell us that we must not work, must not plan ahead. He does not tell us that everything will be done for us. Of course not. But He does tell us that we must not be always worrying and fretting and making a great commotion, as though we, and not He, were responsible for the universe.

"All things are in the hand of God." Have you noticed how the saints always seem to be at their gladdest when things go wrong? And why is it? Surely it is because they have just that faith in the plan, and in the Love that makes the plan. And when there is suffering for them, well, that too is part of the plan, and so to suffer is for them a privilege: it is a part of that total work which is the saving of mankind, the song of love. And so they never waste time and energy brooding over the past or fussing over the future. They live in the present. They get on with the immediate job that God gives them to do, and they leave lovingly in His hands the question of whether it shall be a success or a failure.

They live in the present. So often we forget the importance of each present moment — so fleeting that it seems of no importance, and yet, as we know, it is forever present to the eternity of God, forever present as an act of love and praise, or as a waste and perhaps a betrayal. Live in the present: "At this moment, it is this job, this pain, this joy, that God gives me, so let me make of it as full and deep an act of praise as I can." So you cease to fret and worry, and so you find peace.

⌒

Troubles must not disturb your peace

Sometimes, of course, the job of the moment is the business of coping with worries, but worries are not the same thing as worrying. We cannot escape problems, but if they are God's will for us, well, we can accept them as such and do our best with them without letting ourselves get hopelessly flustered, and the very willing of them *as* God's will can in that case be a kind of peace.

Sometimes it is when we are mere spectators that we find it hardest not to be agitated and not to fret. We see some tragedy impending, and we feel powerless to prevent it. But we must try to see that our fretting is really, in the last resort, a form of egoism, a lack of faith in, trust in, and dependence on God. Our business should be to pray hard (we need never be mere spectators) and then to try to say, "Thy will be done."

Sometimes when we have slowly built up some project that we feel convinced is good — is for God — and then it is wrecked by circumstances outside our control, we want to grumble and to rebel. But no, we should remind ourselves that we never really know, in our tiny glimpse of God's plan, what in the long run is really failure and what is success.

Sometimes it is over ourselves, our own state of soul, that we become agitated in the bad sense. We cannot seem to cope with this or that temptation; we cannot seem to improve. But once again, we must try to live in the present, doing our very best here and now, and neither brooding over our past failures nor letting ourselves sink into a sort of practical despair about the future. All things are in the hands of God.

Once again, it is a question of training ourselves and of starting in small ways. Think of some example of the sort of thing that causes you, individually, to be-come agitated and to fuss. It might be the missing of a train. You are on your way to some important duty, and it seems to be God's will that you should do it. You miss the train, and then you begin to fume and fret. You get into a state, and all to no purpose, whereas you should be telling yourself, "Well, I thought God wanted me to catch the train, but He evidently didn't, and so that's that. If He wants me here, His will be done." And then you could fill in the time by doing something useful instead of pacing up and down the platform like a caged lion, exacerbating your nerves and wasting your time.

~

The Lord constantly watches over you

"Though I should walk in the valley of darkness, yet will I fear no evil: for Thou art with me." There are times when, even though, normally speaking, we have achieved some measure of the sense of God's presence, He seems very remote from us; we seem to be out alone in the dark. It is then, above all, that we need to have trained ourselves to think of events in terms of His will, and to love and accept that will, whatever may fall out.

And in times like these in which we live, how much we need that loving awareness of His watchfulness! We can see only the evil, the suffering, and the despair of the world, and it is hard to believe that out of all that evil any good can come. It is hard not to doubt, hard to trust. But that is just the value of these small and personal beginnings. To be accustomed to see the hand of God — the *loving* hand of God — in all the small events of one's own life, and therefore to go out to meet them, to accept them gladly or at least with loving determination, *because* they are God's will: that is the way to prepare to meet the great things in the same spirit and so to find confidence and peace and happiness in spite of all that can come to disturb and upset us.

The Lord is our Shepherd. Whom shall we fear?

Chapter Five

Let the Our Father draw you closer to God

If we are thinking of the search for God, and in particular of the search for that love of God's will in all things which is the hallmark of holiness and of happiness, we must inevitably think of prayer. And if we begin at the beginning, with the humble, necessary prayer of petition, and go over the lesson our Lord gave us about it, we shall see how important a help this prayer can be.

We might indeed have thought otherwise. Petition, we might have thought, means asking for what *we* want, so it's just the opposite of trying to love and will what *God* wants. But is it?

"Thus shall you pray: 'Our Father . . .' "[17] Let us note, first of all, in passing, that our Lord wants us to

---

[17] Matt. 6:9.

be childlike. Our petition is not to be an offhand statement of our wants, of course. There is the necessary sense of awe, without which our prayer might be something more like a blasphemy.

But, on the other hand, we are not to be unreal; we are not to present an illuminated address. There is no need to indulge in those polysyllabic orotundities that one finds in certain books of devotion. We are to be simple and loving; we are to be like children.

And second, it is "our Father" whom we are to address. Our prayer will not be very good if it is concerned exclusively with ourselves. We have our family to remember, our human family.

⌒

Praise God before you petition Him

"Hallowed by Thy name." We are not to plunge straight into a discussion of our needs and wants. We are not to think of God simply as someone who can supply us with what we want. First we must offer our small gifts, of praise and of love. And if we can offer those, too, not just for ourselves, in our own name, but in the name of all the things and all the people that make up our lives, remembering that they are His and that His presence is about them, so much the better. "Hallowed be Thy name," in and through them all: so we put our prayer that is to follow, and our life as well, on a sure footing. We make our prayer and our life first of all the material of an act of worship.

⤳

Ask for all things according to God's will

"Thy kingdom come": so now reach the prayer of petition, and our Lord shows us clearly how our own needs and wants are to enter into that prayer. Petition is a necessity. It is the proper expression of the creature's dependence on the Creator. We are bound to pray for our needs, and for the needs of our family and of the world. We are allowed to ask God for our wants, but we must see all these things, and especially our own small needs and wants, in their right perspective: I need this and that, but how small those things are in comparison with the terrible needs of the world, and how infinitesimally small in comparison with the total divine plan for the saving of the world from its sin.

"Thy will be done": this is the essence of the whole prayer. Without that clause, our prayer could be a step, not toward God, but away from Him. Sometimes we think we are going to talk to God about X and Y, to praise Him and thank Him for them or to ask Him for some urgent need of theirs, but in reality, we are going to indulge in a good brood about them, with God perhaps vaguely in the background; or we are going to make it quite clear what we want for them, quite forgetting that what is important is what He wants.

"Thy will be done": even when our Lord is reduced to the last extremity of agony — "Let this chalice pass from me"[18] — it is this that He makes the substance of his prayer. It is the same with our Lady at the first great

[18] Matt. 26:39.

turning point of her life: "Behold the handmaid of the Lord."[19]

"Thy will be done" must always be in our prayer, expressed or implied. And it is *because* of this that the prayer of petition is as much a step to union of will with God, and therefore to holiness, as is any other prayer.

One of the most perfect of all the prayers of petition is to be found in the story of the wedding at Cana. "They have no wine,"[20] our Lady said. Love is in no need of windy and wordy rhetoric; love has the simple trust that says, "I know God won't have less love and compassion than I." Love has the sure knowledge that His love and compassion will act — there's no need to shout.

But love also has the modesty — you might say, the heavenly tact — that will not try to thrust itself forward

[19] Luke 1:38.
[20] John 2:3.

when perhaps the thing wanted is not according to God's wisdom. "Your will be done," it says, "for You know best."

And then, at last, our own needs: "Give us our daily bread." It is the symbol for all our needs, bodily and spiritual, and the needs of our human family. There is no reason why we should mention everything explicitly. If we did, we would never be done. Sometimes things weigh on us very much, and then, of course, we want to tell God about them in particular.

But otherwise we are right, once again, to realize that His wisdom knows what we need, and what the world needs, better than we do, and to frame our prayer accordingly.

⸺

Pray with a forgiving heart

"And forgive us our sins, as we forgive others." We know from the psalmist that it is the contrite heart that God does not despise; we know the same thing

50

from our Lord's story of the publican.[21] The sense of our own sin is again a condition of success in our prayer; we shall not be heard if we pray in pride, for the two things are essentially incompatible. But also we cannot expect to be heard and to be helped if we, for our part, turn a deaf ear to calls on our help. "By this shall men know that you are my disciples, if you have love one for another."[22] We cannot pray in the name of Christ unless we are trying to live in the spirit of Christ, forgiving injuries when they are done to us, and listening to cries for help as gladly as we would have God listen to us.

⌒

Recall your dependence on God

And finally, "Lead us not into temptation, and deliver us from evil": once again it is the creature's dependence on God that we are to proclaim. "I have

[21] Luke 18:9-14.
[22] John 13:35.

lifted my eyes to the mountains, from whence help shall come to me."[23] So the Lord's Prayer teaches us to fix our eyes on God, not on ourselves, and to learn to love His will more than our own.

☙

*You can bring a sense of God
to all around you*

The Church teaches us to use the prayer of petition precisely to keep the thought of God's presence with us through the day. It is not at rare isolated moments that we are to pray thus: there are our morning prayers to begin with, then prayers at meals, the *Angelus*,[24] and prayers at night. This frequent recurrence to God is intended to keep us near to Him habitually.

And if, in our petitions, we remember to ask God's blessing on all our work and our interests, our friends,

---

[23] Ps. 120:1 (RSV = Ps. 121:1).

[24] The *Angelus* prayer, which recalls the Incarnation, is traditionally prayed in the morning, at noon, and in the evening.

and all the things that make up our lives, then, again, we are bringing the sense of God into them, and so they in their turn can help to remind us of Him. And if we can form the habit of turning to God momentarily in each need, each duty, and each new problem as it comes, to invoke His help and His blessing, then of course we are really beginning to live with Him in deed, and His presence will begin to color every aspect of our lives.

In that case, we shall begin also to be true "conductors" of His power to the world around us. And that leads us to one final thought. People sometimes think: "If only I could be *doing* something about the suffering and the tragedy of the world, it would be easier to accept it all as part of God's will." The answer is that we can indeed be doing something — something of immense value. First of all, we can pray, and there is no exaggerating the power of really fervent prayer. But we can also turn all our own work, our own trials and troubles, yes, and our joys as well, into a prayer for the world; by taking these as God's will, with love, we can make them a power in the world for peace and love and healing, and so help to bring the world, as well as ourselves, nearer to God.

Chapter Six

Let God's will
permeate all you do

We have been thinking of how we should try to keep our eyes upon God, so as to learn to love and bless His will as it reveals itself from moment to moment, and we have touched on one or two aspects of the life of prayer. There are three points that it may be useful to think of briefly in conclusion.

God forms you through prayer

Prayer is first of all our offering of love and worship to God; it is also one of the chief elements in the process of our formation by God. And from both points of view, we do well to remember the importance of the Church's liturgical life. It enables us to offer ourselves to God totally, body and soul alike, and in the company of the whole of creation.

On the other hand, it enables us to *be formed*, in body and soul alike, nearer to God's ideal for us. We are taught to kneel and stand and walk in the church with reverence for the presence of God; we are taught to look upward to the altar and the tabernacle; we are taught to make the Sign of the Cross, to fold our hands in prayer, and to bow our heads in confession of sin. These things can have a deep effect on the personality: gathering together its forces, unifying it in worship, purifying it, and teaching it candor, humility, uprightness, and love.

The Liturgy appeals to the senses with its sights and sounds and smells, and, again, it is partly as a formative influence on us that these things are important. The senses are appealed to in very different fashion in the manmade world around us, which leads us all too often to disintegration — to a divorce of the sense-life from the life of the spirit, and to the degradation of the senses themselves. We need the Church's Liturgy to restore to us something of our lost unity of body and spirit, and something of the true life of the senses, so that by learning to love truth and goodness and beauty, we may find that the senses help us, instead of hindering and distracting us, in the search for God.

⌒

Meditation deepens your awareness of God's presence

Second, there is the subject of mental prayer. If our share in the Liturgy, our petitions, and our occasional turning of mind and heart to God during the day are to be really and deeply fervent, we need a short period of time set apart every day for mental prayer.

There is no need to be frightened by the words, to suppose that anything grandiose is expected of us. The raising of mind and heart to God, the effort to talk quietly and simply to God, to be with Him and rest quietly in His presence: these are not things that are beyond the reach of the simple, not things to give up as hopeless for us.

Taming the Restless Heart

Some people are helped by simple forms of meditation; others employ brief, spontaneous prayers — aspirations — which they can say over and over again in their hearts for as long as they remain vivid, to bring them close to God. The method is for each individual to decide for himself; the essential is that we should find a way of really becoming aware, in these silent moments, of the presence of God; we should really begin to succeed in that process of "finding and feeling the Infinite," which is the life of prayer and which must go on day by day if is to be effective.

And whether we follow some form of meditation or whether we find the prayer of aspiration more helpful, there is one thing that we can all do with advantage in these times of prayer. It is to tell God, with all the fervor we can command, and with or without precedent meditation on what we say, that we love His will and want to follow it in everything. We cannot mean that fully, no, but never mind. It is good to say the words — "I want to do what *You* want" — and to hope as we say them that they will become more and more true. And if we are faithful in saying them and trying to mean them, they will indeed become more and more true.

◠

*Focusing on God will
allow you to grow in holiness*

The third point is this: suppose you are doing your best to form and inform your mind, your reason, by regular reading of books about God and the life of the spirit. You are doing your best to steep your soul in God day by day in mental prayer. You are letting the Liturgy of the Church mold your sense-life and your intuitive life by its use of symbolism. You are trying to make things redolent of God and to make frequent momentary prayers to God during the day, and so trying to acquire something like a habitual sense of His presence. You are trying, finally, to form a habit of seeing events in the light of His will and His loving wisdom.

What follows? In all these different ways, you are learning to keep your eyes on the Lord, to make Him the most important thing — the center — in your life. And so it will follow that the whole business of the moral life — the business of dealing with temptations and pet vices, of trying to make progress in the virtues — will take on a more theocentric character, for here, too, your eyes will be on the Lord rather than on yourself.

There is always the danger of allowing entrance to the dragon of egoism even into our efforts to serve God better. It is by this means that we can best avert the danger. To say, "*I* must do this and that; *I* must see what progress *I* am making," and so on, is to be egocentric. If you learn to love God enough and keep close to His presence, of course you will want to do better, to cope more effectively with your sins. You will want it far more vehemently than if you were merely to keep looking at yourself, for it is by gazing on His beauty and His purity that we learn to see ourselves as we really are in all our pettiness and squalor. But your whole emphasis will be, not on your own state of soul, but on the way you do His work. It will be His work that matters, and you, for your part, will put your best efforts into being a good tool for that work.

One of the fruits of the Spirit is faithfulness — the sort of fidelity for which we most value the dog. The dog is not always examining its own state of soul, wondering whether it is getting more or less dutiful to its master, going back on unfortunate incidents in the past, or fretting about possible difficulties in the future. Its eyes are indeed on its lord; its whole life is in meeting and responding to his needs and his moods, and doing his work. And in doing that, day by day, the dog does in fact become a part of its master's life, an intimate friend.

That same dogged, unquestioning fidelity, that same immediate full response to the will of the master, is what we, too, need in our life with and for God. It is the fruit of the love that comes from the Spirit, just as peace and joy are fruits of that love, and for the same reason — that it is love that takes one's gaze away from self and fixes it on the goodness and beauty and love of the Beloved.

You can accomplish God's will in small ways

There is so much in the world today to harass us, to fill us with gloom, to tempt us to despair, and, indeed, if we live immersed in the finite, it is difficult to see how despair is to be avoided. But if our mind and heart and will are beginning to be attuned to the rhythm of the Infinite, to breathe Its air, to be formed by It, to feel Its wisdom and Its ceaseless loving care and the vast patient sweep of Its Providence, then despair should be turned into hope and joy and confidence.

We have been thinking of very small things — the simple prayers and acts of worship, the ways of meeting the small difficulties and events of every day — but it is precisely things like these that God wants to use to form us into His likeness. We must not despise or underrate them. Only by fidelity in the small things

can we ever hope to be able to do anything great:
"Well done, good and faithful servant. Because thou
hast been faithful over a few things, I will place thee
over many things. Enter thou into the joy of thy
Lord."[25]

[25] Matt. 25:21.

Biographical Note

Gerald Vann, O.P.

(1906-1963)

Born in England in 1906, Gerald Vann entered the Dominican Order in 1923 and, after completing his theological studies in Rome, was ordained a priest in 1929. On returning to England, he studied modern philosophy at Oxford and was then sent to Blackfriars School in Northhamptonshire to teach and later to serve as headmaster of the school and superior of the community there. Tireless in his efforts to bolster the foundations of peace, he organized the international Union of Prayer for Peace during his tenure at Blackfriars.

Fr. Vann devoted his later years to writing, lecturing, and giving retreats in England and in the United States, including giving lectures at The Catholic University of America in Washington, D.C.

He wrote numerous articles and books, including a biography of St. Thomas Aquinas, who influenced him greatly. Fr. Vann's writings combine the philosophy and theology of St. Thomas with the humanism emphasized in the 1920s and 1930s. His works reflect his keen understanding of man's relationship to God, his deep sensitivity to human values, and his compassionate understanding of man's problems and needs. Particularly relevant in today's divided world is his appeal for unity, charity, and brotherhood. His words reveal what it means today to fulfill the two greatest commandments: to love God and to love one's neighbor.

Sophia Institute Press®

Sophia Institute is a nonprofit institution that seeks
to restore man's knowledge of eternal truth, including
man's knowledge of his own nature, his relation to
other persons, and his relation to God.

Sophia Institute Press® serves this end in numerous
ways: it publishes translations of foreign works to make
them accessible for the first time to English-speaking
readers; it brings out-of-print books back into print;
and it publishes important new books that fulfill the
ideals of Sophia Institute. These books afford readers
a rich source of the enduring wisdom of mankind.

Sophia Institute Press® makes these high-quality
books available to the general public by using advanced
technology and by soliciting donations to subsidize its
general publishing costs. Your generosity can help

Sophia Institute Press® to provide the public with editions of works containing the enduring wisdom of the ages. Please send your tax-deductible contribution to the address below. We also welcome your questions, comments, and suggestions.

For your free catalog, call:
Toll-free: 1-800-888-9344

or write:
Sophia Institute Press®
Box 5284, Manchester, NH 03108

or visit our website:
www.sophiainstitute.com